John,
Merry Christmas "
Happy New Year!
Bob

ROBERT SZANKOWSKI

SWIMMING LESSONS

A FREESEEKER PUBLICATION

FOREWORD BY CARA DE LUNA

ILLUSTRATIONS AND COVER BY ERIKA

Copyright © by freeseeker Publishing Company

ISBN-13: 978-1519733504
ISBN-10: 151973350X

All rights reserved. No part of this book may be reproduced in any form or by any means, electronic or mechanical, including photocopying and recording, or by any information storage and retrieval system, without permission in writing from the Publisher.

CONTENTS

FOREWORD by Cara de Luna / ix

SWIMMING LESSONS

WORDS OF ADVICE / 3
ON INDIFFERENCE / 4
ON COMPASSION AND FEAR / 5
TEN COMMANDMENTS OF LOVE / 6
ON BEING REPLACABLE / 8
ON DESIRE / 9
A PERSONAL FAVOR / 10

AS LONG AS I REMEMBERED, I REMEMBERED
of no significance / 15
With Words / 16
Three Haiku / 17
impermanent poem / 18
Missing Poem / 20
Night Jasmine / 22
Panoramic / 24
A Kiss of Orpheus / 25
Bleed! / 26
Hatchling / 28
A Name Already Known / 30
As a Kiss / 32
Why? / 34

THE LANGUAGE OF STRANGERS
Walk With Me / 41
this is what I want / 42
Debt / 44
Out of the Wild / 46
An Irish Song / 49
My First Language / 50
In Praise of a Woman / 52
a more human love / 55
courtship / 56
mutual propinquity / 58
Savannah Spring / 60
In Spite of Space / 62
another paradise / 64
The Shape of Love / 66
that night / 68
another night / 69

THE DARK CENTERS OF EYES
nirvana / 73
the notebook *with Cara de Luna* / 74
Midnight Poem / 76
He Must / 78
Meditation / 80
joy *with Cara de Luna* / 81
lilium / 82
Out of Eden (Pandora Atones) / 84
Organized / 86
Hello. / 88
Hollow / 90
Machine Dreams / 92
life / 95
the offering / 96
Let Me Find Ways *with Cara de Luna* / 98
s t r e t c h / 101

EVERY PATH IS THE RIGHT PATH
Mission Statement / 105
Sonnet X / 106
Sonnet XI / 107
Sonnet XII / 108
The Fountain / 110
Light Poem / 112
The Old Folks Know / 113
A New Home / 114
All the Bright Colors / 117
locked to life / 120
Unwasted / 123
River / 124
The Candle / 126
Lighthouse / 127
Discovery / 128
Dining / 130
a drop of water / 131
getting up / 132
Can't you see me smiling? / 134
Dharma in a Bag / 135
swimming lessons *with Cara de Luna* / 136
Open Letter / 140
walk to walk / 142

FOREWORD

I often ask myself if what I am contributing to the world is enough. And on certain afternoons, like this one, when the sunset is a soft yet vibrant red, I find myself contemplating flowers. Why? Because flowers are enough, for they simply *are,* like poetry.

I remember when I first connected with Robert we discovered we shared a similar passion for poetry, for creating something beautiful and meaningful for others to be inspired by. This marked the beginning of a creative collaboration, which I did not know at the time, would lead to the creation of *Swimming Lessons.* It is an honor to have taken part in the growth of a project with a writer that knows where he wants to go with his art. We both feel the language of poetry speaks beyond time and culture, and it is with great hope when we create something with essence, that it will light fires in the minds and hearts of people.

I recall the day when Robert asked me if I wanted to collaborate on a poem. I was both surprised and a little apprehensive. I asked myself, "What could I possibly contribute to his poetry?" In my view, I felt his poetry was already a clear blue sky, concise and well-formed; and I was afraid I'd make a sludge of his crystalline structures that are his poems. I admit, my writing is like a moonlit river, and the lines blur, and I flit from abstract to realism and back again, forever in a perpetual see-saw motion of, what may appear as indecision, but which I take to be as, the exploration of the mutable and emotively mercurial realms. I am aware I am shapeless, in search of shape, but not quite owning it once it's found it, for I go back to an impressionistic shapelessness to form something new again. Robert's poetry is akin to the mastering of the sculptor's knife, which creates a piece that leads the reader to imbue a message. This is, what I believe, art's ultimate goal is in general; to pass on a message. I feel there must be clarity of purpose, and Robert's poetic expression embodies this.

Nevertheless, I agreed to a collaborative poem - I still felt I could bring something despite my doubts.

When our first poem, *swimming lessons*, came into form, I was amazed! The ideas had fluidly moved from mind to words as we wrote it together, it was almost a seamless train of creative flow. My mutable swiftness somehow worked when it came into contact with his solid shapes. I really felt something was being formed, despite my initial doubts about my ability. I admired Robert's clarity, and like I said before, I was afraid to make a mess of his structures.

But the formation of our first poem had trumped all of my doubts, and when we worked on more poems together I felt more confident. We soon found that the dynamic and creative energy in our collaborative poems was taking us somewhere.

I am honored to have contributed to *Swimming Lessons,* and to have had the opportunity to collaborate with a talented writer such as Robert. He is a passionate soul with a clear voice and strong spirit, who both understands beauty and sensitivity, while seeking to break societal and cultural barriers with his art. This collaborative journey and friendship with Robert has led me to see once again how dynamic it is when minds come together to create, especially if there is a common vision shared.

To inspire others is, I believe, at the core of artists. And the spirit of collaboration is a powerful force in the world that needs to be tapped into more. I feel *Swimming Lessons* is but one manifestation of this force, it not only expresses the need in me to create with a like-minded artist, but it is my hope that the poetry you discover within the pages of this book will ease in and out of your mind the way water moves, making the flowers in your mind blossom; and ultimately, leading you to be inspired to contemplate some soft thought or novel idea.

Do not be afraid to *seek* beauty and to express your passion *for* beauty. Write about it if you must, for poetry is enough, by simply *being* poetry, in a world that seeks light.

Thank you for taking the time to be inspired.

Cara de Luna

WORDS OF ADVICE

There are some who live life by waiting for it to offer them the right opportunity, the right moment, the right feeling. This is no way to achieve anything in life. No one on their deathbed says I wish I waited a bit more for the right offer, closed myself to something, protected my feelings a bit more.

Then there are some who grab life, shake it up, take it all in, and scream about it at the top of their lungs. These people seek and seek and seek with a free love for all the beauty in this world in such a way they will continue to grow as long as they live. They are an excitable and affectionate bunch. With them, sometimes there is magic and sometimes there is not. This makes them vulnerable and prone to being hurt. When this happens their sadness gives them strength and does not cause them to cower away with their darkness, or hide it away with a façade. They embrace their pain. They stay strong because they have loved without love in return so much that eventually this type of love makes them powerful, because they have brought virtue into their disappointment to let it shine.

No one defines you but yourself. No one makes you happy but yourself. Learn from your sadness, use it, love it, create with it, bring it into your happiness. Do not hide it away or numb it. It is part of you. This sadness is part of life, its pain is inevitable, but the suffering is optional. Do not be afraid to be disappointed or saddened, that is suffering, instead be courageous. The more you give, the more love gathers. Don't let the world tell you who you are. Tell the world who you are, say I'm here, and I am coming whether you like it or not.

ON INDIFFERENCE

Nothing is never indifferent. Nothing is quite the opposite, the great blank space of the void, where all of existence springs from, the birthplace of stars, of oceans and skies, of trees and water, of the great and terrible loves. It is the great canvas which everything is painted onto: the music, the sights, the feelings. Indifference is a human thing; it is a façade which fights the quintessential reason we are alive, to love and be loved.

Indifference hides away emotions, it tucks them away where no one can see them, it ignores suffering, it is scared of love, it fights the need to be an ever creating person. Indifference is not how you treat another; it is how you treat yourself. We all deserve the feelings we feel, we all deserve to feel happy, to feel angry, to feel sad.

Do not confuse balance with indifference. Being mindful of our emotions brings us balance; it knows sadness is a beautiful thing which helps us grieve loss in a healthy way. While indifference is like a drug which covers the sadness only to be never fully expressed and eventually sinks us deeper into depression. Balance controls emotions, while indifference lets emotions control. Life is to be filled, not to be hidden away. Indifference is a lie. And for whatever reasons, whether social pressures, self-centered pride, indifference is a war you fight with yourself in fear of the deep down real you.

ON COMPASSION AND FEAR

When a squirrel sees you it runs in fear because it thinks you will harm it. But are you? Humans work this way too; this is why there is war, hunger, untreated disease, suffering, blame, and a lack of personal responsibility. There is a profit motive in this instinct of fear, it is a machine which continually manifests itself into the media you watch on television, the magazines which tell you who to be, and the bombardment of hate and fear you see even on your Facebook feed. This is why we are so complacent and expect others to solve our problems. Break this machine today.

Humans though, have a capacity for compassion. Through good deeds, philosophy, art there are those who will make every attempt to break down barriers, bring people together, and create a world where people can understand each other and most importantly themselves. They do this not by telling you who to be, but telling you their own experience and reflecting it to the world. They are not saying buy this and you will be happy, they are saying understand with me on this and perhaps we can make a better world by being brothers and sisters.

Compassion trumps fear. When we fear we do not let things happen in our life, we lock our doors, we shut people down; we close our emotions to each other. This is an instinct, no doubt. But we have evolved to the point where we can understand ourselves and the choices we make. We have the knowhow to know when we are making a choice whether out of fear or compassion. In the end it is not what you see, it is what you want to see. Truly "look at" and "understand" the world around you and together WE WILL make this world a better place.

TEN COMMANDMENTS OF LOVE

1. Do not fight for love. Just love. Love does not demand, it does not expect, it does not desire for someone to give to you; this is attachment. Give without expecting anything in return. Love without expecting love in return.

2. When you think of words or actions which will make someone happy, say it and do it.

3. The saying "everything happens for a reason" has nothing to do with what happens to you from the outside. Do not be a victim. There are no mistakes in life, there is only a one way street which springs from the self. When you walk around being a victim you always will be just that.

4. Understand there will be ups and downs in life. If you keep the road level, it will always be straight and mundane. The best parts of life are uncertain. Without sadness, there is no joy. Take your time to grieve, understand melancholy is a beautiful experience, and with these reflective moments we bring ourselves greater joy.

5. Ask questions to others and to yourself. There is always something to be learned and understood, especially when you ask yourself. Reflect and meditate on the answers. Let them guide you to the true you.

6. Treat the present moment as if it is a door to both the past and the future. Everything in life is now, the future and past depend on how you open and close these doors.

7. Do not be frustrated when you are misunderstood. Everyone has their own life to venture, do not push yourself on people committed to misunderstanding you. True friends will take their time to understand you. Observe this and embrace this. These are the people you want to surround yourself with.

8. Listen.

9. Be honest about who you are. Do not try to impress someone with something you have no interest in doing or being. Not only are you lying to them, but more importantly to yourself. Be genuine with your passion, it will spill when it spills.

10. See the beauty in imperfections. Everyone has brokenness about them. Perfect is boring, it is the imperfections which are the most interesting and attractive. These struggles, blemishes and heartaches are things which make others admirable, inspiring and moving. Our imperfections are where our light shines out. Let it shine and light up the world with love.

ON BEING REPLACEABLE

You have the heard the saying: "everybody is replaceable". But this only applies to the practical world. Sure, grocery clerks, construction workers, plumbers, lawyers, doctors, bartenders and politicians are all replaceable. These are not people; these are things people do to a make a living. What defines a person is not how they make a living, it is how they live; it is their dreams and passions, the way they touch another, the way they gaze at and paint the sky, the way they comfort, and the way they smile, what they do in their life when it's not about putting food on the table or a roof over their head. This is the way a person is unique. This is how people are irreplaceable.

No one can ever replace a Monet or a John Lennon, because they put their living in their life, not their life in their living. They offered their heart and soul on a platter to the world, and no one else felt and loved quite like they did. Each and every one of you have something to offer no else can imitate, something no one can feign or put in a prepackaged box to be sold to the masses.

It is when you buy what is broadcast over the airwaves, when you live life according to others, and when you live a life which is deemed to be socially practical and familiar that we are replaceable. Any man or woman can put food on the table; any person can do the things everyone else is already doing. But to be truly unique and truly irreplaceable you must offer something no one else can, something that is uniquely your own, this is the deep down you; this is the reason people fall in love with you. This is why it is important to embrace what may make you weird, or different

Some may not like you, since you are not quite what has been sold to them all their life, but there will be someone who let you in and from that moment forward they will know it is only from you that they will receive what you are offering. We are all born artists; we are all born to be a unique creation of our own.

ON DESIRE

When we focus our thoughts on something, whether it is something we desire or something we would want to break free from, we attract this energy to ourselves. If you desire to not desire, you will still desire. Everything we attract is in direct influence from what we think, whether negative or positive. When you focus on something you do not want you are giving this thing strength and power over you, just as you would if you focused on something you do want. Be present in your moment and let it unfold, do not focus so much on things out of your control, and be positive with your thoughts; become and evolve rather than reduce and remain.

A PERSONAL FAVOR

Do yourself a favor and look at life, look at the stars, read poetry, dance to music and be present with each movement, immerse yourself in the ideas which transcend all which is beautiful and sad and inspirational. Life is not ordinary, we are here to make it grand, we are here to love. This is a gift. Embrace it.

As Long as I Remembered,

I Remembered

of no significance

the waters murmur in morning air;
    it is an insignificant event,
    but for me it is everything.
how the tides push
into roots of live oaks
curved towards dawn,
and how it won't
go into the annals
of great battles and treks.
yet I am here,
    it is true,
and before this
I was somewhere else
just as Hilton
was before he named
this island.

these trees have seen
more than I have,
many storms,
many critters
nuzzling their skin.
above me there is a spider
making its web;
    its expertise is certified.
and here I walk,
no other human but me
    and I am
no longer sure
of what is important.

With Words

We are born with wild eyes
without words, only
blinking for the sky
wishing, dreaming, loving
everything: the faces
with smiles, the color blue,
sonatas standing up and walking,
carrying flags towards the stars
erupting into life.

And we learn words, their shape,
their color, and how they explode,
how they can destroy and create
everything: the faces afraid
to lose, the lyrics breaking
apart music manipulating
the listeners to turn
away from the melody.

It takes a lot to know men
and women. It takes a lot
to walk across the islands
in our dust making shadows
we stand inside and keep
our flags in our eyes.

It takes a lot to love.

But we do.

Three Haiku

Old coloring book
dust over yellow paper
  Absent crayon marks

Summer ends
 no honey bee hums
Parched still wings

  Cigarette finds fire
street lamps illuminate
Moved by silent words

impermanent poem

tonight
I want to write
the words
which are set afire
as you read them.

they will hold
the secret
of the universe.
into ash
and into air,

each syllable
vanishing
before your eyes.
you will learn
to take care

of each one,
to taste them
and chew them.
you will
nurture every sound

on the tip
of your tongue,
breathe their smoke
into your streams
of blood.

feel them
as a warm waterfall
of stars
pouring
from the moon

into the ocean
of your unseeing sight
where each atom glows
into the warmth
at the ends

of your fingers,
to the edge
of your toes,
to the red flesh
of your lips.

walk with them,
touch with them,
kiss with them.
feel them dance
in your chest

inside
and about you,
where now only
will they ever
reside.

Missing Poem

I wrote a poem
for everyone,
it was about beauty
and life,
love
and strength.
It was
about the faces
and places
bitten with rain and fire,
the big job, the ladders
to Mars.

It talked about how
mornings look like young people,
how they yawn
into the air
and in an instant
bring energy
into all the dark
corners of the earth.

It mentioned
all the different ways
we say
"I am here"
and
"touch me."

It did math
with odd and even numbers,
and proved prime ones
were always odd.
It showed
how the slope
of the land
bended to the curves
of our bodies,
how they comfort us
and teach us,
challenge us to look beyond
its hard
yet tender surface.

But now
I seem
to have misplaced it.
If you find it
make sure
to read it
and write your own,
you do not need a pen
or a typewriter.

No need
to return it to me,
you are welcome
to though,
or you can
just lose it like me
for someone else
to find.

Night Jasmine

You spring around me
like clusters of stars

in the early autumn night.
And when daylight comes,

you fade but not before
the taste of your mouth

and the color of your skin
lift up from your roots

into your arms holding me
on the earth I water every day.

Because every time I wake
to continue my journey

you disappear like the aroma
which never blossoms into fruit,

only to fall to the ground
making room for the next moon.

For when the night comes again
and you release your dust

holding your scent,
it will lead me back to you.

Panoramic

She says: "morning comes
with coffee"
and we sit at the bay
window where we can see
finches leap from branch
to branch and watch the Sunday
traffic towards gospels and eggs.

We hide our hands under
the table and touch fingers
and knees, and we smile
tiny sips bringing us
closer to our parting day
upon the earth we both
know, brief with stillness
shaking the wind.

I hold my thoughts in the flavor
of her mouth and the shade of her
skin, and how it has been with
the earth for some time, how
we both know the sound of rain
and how saplings turn into trees.

Yet our words are of our mothers
and fathers, the climbing
of childhood and university,
the faith of our mountains,
the swerving air we both breathe.

A Kiss of Orpheus

wanted much more than a taste
of ruminations of divine wine
and the fate of Shakespeare

no need to tame this shrew

she already feels the violence
of stonewalls
and how they can torment
sensational men into madness

she showed me
her Mercury
as I felt her chic melancholy,
a confounded transition

my bare ring finger caressed
with breathed prophecies
as I gave her a message
to her lips
tracing the infinity
of a bigger bang
that only for that moment
she would
know

Bleed!

The angels were singing
ahs, ohs, oms and oohs
as the rock 'n'
roll records my dad
would play on a Sunday
afternoon. "You Can't
Always Get What You
Want" but you could
find secret tunnels
to the howl beating
in another's great
solitude. There is
an echo there rolling,
circulating like in veins,
these tunnels turning
blood into words into
stone preserving
un-kissed lips and New
York City subway rides.
Bleecker Street, The Bitter
End, nope, just the trumpet
sound of bop jazz preaching
the word buzzing
in a closed mouth. Oh God,
the blare! My eyes
are heavy, no tears,
just beauty pulled towards
the single passenger
taxi cab talk with
Vladimir from Russia,
he has a wife, two kids,
and loves America. Slam!

The door closes, stampede
about, I need a drink,
the planet is sobbing
and I cannot do anything
about it, maybe more blood
and a Jack and Coke. This
will get the fingers
moving, grab the pen, stab
yourself in the chest,
it is a minor surgery,
there it is pumping,
feeling.
Now bleed.

Hatchling

A crow has learned to crow today,
a pure caw for nourishment,
letting the world know he is alive,
letting his mother know he needs her;
he left his perfect egg-shell
and now naked and blind
he starts to learn
this nest is not his home.

A Name Already Known

We keep on naming the babies
   all the names
  we already know
     and nothing happens.

Everything circles around,
   drifting together,
              swimming apart,
  combined and remixed
     into hip hop parades crawling from
     the black and white past
     into the color that exploded
     from Hiroshima's song demanding
     a bended knee from Apollo,
        illuminating
        the quadrilateral
        digest inside
        the platonic dialogue
        climbing the fire escape
        towards Mars.

And Blake is still
making the divine image
out of the human form
as if we are martyrs
all burning together
with a single yawn
waiting to sleep together
in the orgy between the sky.

We dream
    and have no glory,
waiting for the next
    reincarnation
       where we will not remember
          as we wake again
          to a new light of dawn
          with a name already known.

As a Kiss

In this poem
I kiss you
when I am not near.

It came
from inside me
where my kiss
is hidden
away from hidden things,

where it shines
like a candle.

Read it aloud
and feel the wax drip
from my fingers
as the heat rises
to your mouth
now a song
of our tangled tongues.

Touch your lips
and feel how my words
are the way I add
up the air breathed
into your air,
each stress
a beat
which chronicles
the lightning bolts
of your upward smile,
each relaxed sound
filling the melody
of my reddish skin
tempting the complete circle
of your gaze.

Why?

Why the loud daily
thundering?
The clouds rolling
above hiding
the stars, which come
one by one,
getting closer
day by day
from another
world to imagine.

As long as I
remember,
I remembered
the morning,
the wind,
the color blue,
the aloneness
of childhood
bedrooms,
the sound
of a throat
filling the air
with the things
which make cathedrals
and books.

My father,
for a while,
answered every why,
and my mother
did not
write poems.
But they roused them
in a mind
of a boy
who did not
yet question
the Catholic
school jump rope lessons.

I was safe with them.

Lessons coalesced
into a Strauss like
crescendo
long before
I spoke,
and the rain came
cascading
with the wind.
I was covered
in holy water
and still in a day
without a name.

I was late to love
and was dropped
from heights
so high,
I learned how
to make wings
out of pen and paper.

Apparently,
I had faith
in the words
covered in colors
and shapes
of my memories.
And now I write
poems
which have come the whole way.

The Language of Strangers

Walk With Me

When the Earth
holds the last light
of evening
it is as two hands
releasing their grip
only to touch slightly
the hairs upon each
finger.

Could we go there,
could we meet
at the border of our island,
walk along
its edge
and over its softness?

I want to see where
our naked feet
may lead
and listen to time roll
below the silent
fire in the sky.

this is what I want

to transform the eyes
of a stranger
with a dirty joke
or some wine.

to lose and find myself
in the sound
of another, their laugh,
their shiver

when they know they are
no longer alone.

to anticipate stars
to turn nightly
in an empty mind
bemused to love,

they would tire if not.

to learn again how to touch,
to cover
blankets over the night

and not think of what
it all means
or when
it all ends.

what a beautiful thing
this would be.

their dance the same
as my dance,
within me, before me
all along.

Debt

I am
in debt
to those
I do not
know.

They give me
so much freedom,
so much peace;
friendship does
not offer
this.

I do not have
to be patient
with them,
I am not
expecting
them to smile
and say hello,
or ask
how everything
is.

I do not
need to make
apologies for
the long pauses
of nothingness
between
us.

I owe
them nothing,
yet for them
I have
my empty
hands
waiting
with love.

Out of the Wild

Perhaps it will be your hair
springing out of the roots
of your dreams
around your pale neck
towards your caring bosom,
like a waterfall pouring
into the lagoon
where I drink
your sweet solitude.

It will be only I
who witness this
in this human jungle,
a piece of earth
not yet utterly sought
even by the adventurous men
who must touch every landscape.

There
I will graze your surface
as a parched jaguar
feeling your cool wet
soften my lips.
I will look into
your mist climbing out
of the splash of your eyes,
refracting light
into all the colors
of Autumn.

I will search behind
this cascade
carefully along the slippery stones
for the hidden grotto
where I will rest
as day passes,
and gaze in your reflection
into the night sky
while your waters
drown the noise
of the wild.

An Irish Song

She told me I can find her
in a library or a painting,
the places where beats
are not attached to rhyme.

The still settings waiting
to be filled with shouting
and laughter with Irishmen
swaying side to side;

James Joyce and Bram Stoker,
C.S. Lewis and Oscar Wilde
with pints overflowing, singing
"Oh Danny Boy", and no one
can hear them outside.

She said: "They are
waiting too in an adventure
and every page has a surprise,
and their hearts turn like yours
with dreams
folded into desires;

I know it's hard when no one listens
when all you want to do is give what is inside,
but I will be here waiting
when that still night comes alive."

My First Language

The language of poetry
was not my first language.
I once spoke with unclosed eyes
before they opened between
the mountains and the sea
where white clusters rose
beyond the waves
like shipwrecked sailors,
lost in an unwritten history,
sent out to find the women
who sing songs
for hearts stopped
by hands made for stone.

And now they have finally
found their way
to my fingers
which hold the soft sand
to let it
fall with the wind.
I breathe the salt-air
into lungs, into veins
and it sings for the sky,
for the branching orange trees
and their golden sweetness.

Only a handful of earth
separates each of us, the opaque
walls of only a few miles
soaked in the morning
of bluebirds.
I was born in this fire
lying between an ocean
and another and I cried
at the distance until I saw
night was also aflame.

My wild beauty, we walked
backwards to retake time
measured in the miles
between kiss before kiss.
I am the vine winding
around a dead pine,
oh how vain my insides are
without life to hold me.

My outward grapes are how I touch
your lips. Taste me.
All love is inside
each love my dear,
all arid mouths are made wet
with each embrace,
and each night meets
the light of each day.
And here, we will meet
where we will have forgotten
nothing.

In Praise of a Woman

Every time I close my eyes
I can see

the lines of her mouth
and how they arch
towards the hiddenmost
tissue behind my face

pointed towards the skies
where my heart dances
like blood and alcohol
mixed in the vessels between;
and how they fall,
rise up
on fire,

and how
in this stare,
I will allow her
to see myself
fragile
like music

coming from a Spanish guitar
played in a rain soaked alleyway
patrolled by the gestapo
suppressing the freedom
in the song of my love.

Oh how strong a woman must be?

She wanders through this slippery
pavement not aware

of the callused hands
wanting to touch softly
and place inside her bosom
the oceans which hold
the ships with the cargo
of my churning flesh;

so bright the vista,
so loud the waves
at this dawn,
at these beaches
where she contemplates
if this is where
she had always been
to go on
with me.

a more human love

it is
the rhythm of solitude,
the greatest undertaking
between two souls,

not to
crumble absent barriers
but to reveal distance
as closeness, togetherness,
without shadow, always opening
the spaces full of life

and growth, where we find
each other as the everlasting
fireworks display against the sky,
immeasurable in perpetual discovery

that we kiss
and touch and hold
with the firmness of earth
with both original loves
learned from each
aloneness

where we give
and not lose the gift of our
finest possession

courtship

there is something to learn
from every courtship
through silences
and gazes, through kisses
and chats of needs

only fools can take
a woman with affection
to where immortality is lethal,
where touch is exact
and words are taught
secondhand

I watch breaths
fill women's curves in night
and if only I show
curiosity will they touch
me
or I touch
them

at times
I can carry
a tune and listen,
always wanting
to dance

I can talk of ex-boyfriends,
ex-husbands, hobbies and flowers,
upbringings and values;
nothing perfect,
perhaps excellent
like sex
always gauged by fantasies

we learn fast of limits
and boundaries,
the former tenants of desires;
the lines to be crossed or followed
when patience becomes
no reason to be content

mutual propinquity

funny how the truth never comes in waiting
how it hits you at a happy hour
in some unsuspecting voice
saying: "Excuse me, did I hear that right!?"
but those are just words
that brought to my attention your hands
inspected for any trace of bondage
away from concentrated fuck-me eyes
immersed in a grin cleaner than water

Savannah Spring

A human roar looks like allure
in city markets little past noon;
a wink of circumstance,
connection to take or not take
to the river of current without
certain understanding of you.

An echo in its depths, sonar
like a pulse getting closer with
each exchange of quietness
as pings morph into words,
and words into movement.

I am in debt from those who left
me crying before, high
rises next to old churches and
the pieces I learned from them.

Yet did I know of
your sweat that would
drip into my pores,
replacing tears. Yet did I know
suppleness of your breasts,
your unspoken tongue talking
to me with shared taste.

Because of the clearness
of this first day and distant
shadows of clouds we
watched in the horizon
with lightning foreshadowing
our magnetism with earth;

and I asked you to dance
when the storm found
our brows, but I settled for a kiss
when we read the words inscribed
on a rain covered relic of past.

In Spite of Space

Dawn tapped me on the shoulder
at midnight and her smile was full
of a thousand sheets of paper.
So much to be filled, so much
between: us, her lips, the gaps
between her teeth wanting to bite
into the morning air.

Her tresses flew
in her melody filled vibration
supported by her long legs
swaying to the rhythm
of the space separating her
from me.

Serenading her
in uncertain words, the language
of strangers sharing the seas
and the earth, I did not know
whether it was around us or in
the middle where I
opened the door to the sound
of her music

another paradise

Monday morning,
8:55 AM,
my car
stopped
at a red light.

To my left,
a middle aged man
smoking monotony
and smothered
in life insurance.
He is driving
a Jeep Wrangler
covered in the mud
of a weekend excursion.

To my right,
a good-looking
weary woman
in a white minivan
with an empty baby seat
in tow.
She glances over
and I smile,
she smiles back
and brushes her hair
with her bare left hand.

Green light turns
and things
start moving again,
but I stay still
for a couple more moments
until horns blast me
into another paradise.

The Shape of Love

After I read
my first love story,
I went looking for
your eyes, not understanding
how I was blinding
my eyes and yours.

I took sight away
from the avenue
which sprawls all
of the fragrant blossoms
and the winding roads
to each side of my fated
feet not acknowledging
the adventure.

I have let my body
be an inn and not
a world with no end.
The whole is the holiday,
a revolving ball
of everlasting color and sound
to be filled with touches
and tastes.

Yet I searched for another
dimension, another life,
not knowing
it is here I belong,
it is here I wanted to be
before I came into this.

I am a sapphire held up
to the rays, through
me I refract the blueness
of skies, the poetry
which knocks on the door
with laughter inside
which forms the rivers
and oceans of affection
sprung from the ache
singing for each day.

The shape of my love
forms to the container
it is poured in, and you will
feel it, and test it with
your little toes, scoop it in
a cup, and we will both
drink it
and let the current
take us.

that night

that night
was an overflowing goblet,
that night was a shared star
burning in our eyes, that night
it was all the sky

on the pier
stretched over the bay
as it held us to kiss
over ripples, so close
to water, we felt them rush
into each other
forming larger waves, we
watched them without letting go

before we walked back towards
the earth and looked back
to watch the wet moon
pour a single drop
into the horizon

and beyond us
a curtain had lifted
and something shapeless
was still
there

another night

the air was clear and cool
and our bellies were full
with wine and we walked
hand in hand towards the edge
of the ocean

the moon was conducting
the roar of the tide
as we looked over its waves
as we focused on the sound
of its foam fizz and fade
at our toes

the sky had not changed
much since we first kissed
by the still waters
on the quiet side of our island

yet our lips were familiar
strangers now and this night
was without prejudice

The Dark Centers of Eyes

nirvana

all of time
    in a carafe,
    I pour it inside
    me
until
    there is
    no me,
until
    all is
nowhere,
everywhere

the notebook

unwritten,
    untouched,
unspoiled by emotional landscapes
to form in the dusk
of desire inside my silhouette.
I observe its solitude;
pale blue lines
    begin to twirl and blur
along with the awkward wire
that spirals into the holes
on the edge of its canvas.

the lines laugh and disintegrate -
   only the off white voidness pulls me
towards each turn of my weaving thoughts;
        and suddenly,
I find myself in a new space to feel free.

the pages waltz, undressed of any limitation,
naked in their revelry, and I careen with them
in the only way I know when I am not bound.

it demands five subjects, yet
I want only to express one,
I put it down in the west reaches
in its upper hemisphere;
it is in the shape of a star
pulsating within the ocean of whims covering
my artistry like a blanket
   above the first page of its sky.

I watch it

    * burn and burn and burn *

    and

    e x p l o d e

  into a supernova,

* a brilliant spark of zeal *

the once empty paper is reborn into a fused factory of words;
    my imagination is formed into a universe
coloring and filling with music, touching and tasting
the stardust of my dreams.

Midnight Poem

Every midnight
a new day
is created
under black

blankets with
specks radiating
remnants of
previous hours.

They invite
you to view
the past --
and command

the dark centers
of eyes
to widen to all
the brilliant islands

reflecting on
the long lagoon
where the moon
makes a path

to the edge
of your heart.
If it is your nature
to be daring,

to be a dreamer
on this hour,
your imagination
will find all

it needs: the croaks,
the whistles, the shrieks,
the wind shaking trees
playing music

to the sparse traffic
on the distant parkway.
In all of this
there is a man

coming home
to a woman
who will be told
she is not

loved anymore.
So keep on walking,
somewhere in your depths
an angel is singing

the earth knew precisely
what it wanted --
from the stars
igniting your mind on fire.

He Must

He wakes early
since the swallows
are singing
outside his window.
He wants to sing with them
and he does
in his mind
with closed eyes.
He is
laughing in the trees.

He has no answer,
only a song,
it hums deep
inside his feathered
breast, it is thrust
into the air
through his aching
flesh where he was touched
by the sharp edge
of the world.

Meditation

Close your eyes, now listen
to the sounds: a cough, a sneeze,
the motors rumbling around, the squirrels
climbing the long trunks, birdsongs
fluttering inside the sunlight; you
cannot unidentify all of this even
with your sight shut. You cannot
try to, no meditation can do this,
know and accept this. Now breathe,
notice how you were already.

joy

the wind passes through the music
of your breath
and clouds rejoice
with the light reflected off the moon

you can see it
as waves topple to hug your toes
on the golden sands like a trumpet
celebrating the remaining days of summer

you feel the vibration, the moment,
the glow of earth inside you
as the day opens

you try to grasp it, hold it, own it,
when you do
it runs away with the wind

you tremble and your knees kiss the ground
then minivans arrive,
they pour out a symphony
of blossoms
laughing at the sun

lilium

you
fall
back
and your body
faces
the sky

within closed eyes
your memories
are like lush brown
crowned
with stargazers

I
want
to climb
into your darkness
and smell
the flowering
locks

the cascade of perfumed novae

each one
creating
a rebirth
in fingers
unearthing
the starry nights of summer

Out of Eden (Pandora Atones)

Not much more than a child,
a sleeping skeleton surrounded
in meat and cloth and furniture,
animated with emptiness,
the accident of the industrious
fire, the clouds billowing out
of the sea. I is the name,
a renewed sorrow, discovered joy.

I counts, I scratches, I marches,
I grows out of earth, out of I,
and I bamboozles I preaching I
is separate from I. And the torch
is given by the sick, the dying
without profit in unrecorded treks
towards placid commonwealths
and blankets covering lovers
of their own morning.

Meanwhile, disease conquers,
species go extinct, temples
burned in political worlds
and the ashes stowed away
in the nearest bank where
stairwells are long. Our flesh
is a reservoir of suffering,
and it has to rest, to eat,
breathe, and it did this
before and after Christ.

The run of rivers change
and trees rot back to Earth,
all giving. And our lid is
loose uncertain by its own
existence, having nowhere to
go, nothing to do, happy
from time to time, spared
with the gift of never
seeing too far off into
the future.

Organized

Feeling is first, it is not
about the words, life is not
a manuscript. There were whole
acres in America that never
heard a single word. No one
lived there, morning was unseen
and it was not given a name.
Then it seemed to come out
of nowhere: the crying,
the laughter, the complete
childhood, and how the gorgeous
women made the body twitch.
And we had to call it something,
like soft or warm, lavender
or infinite. What madness
drove us to put touch in a book?
Pleasures would be better without
the structured noise we hang
on the automatic novelties made
into shapely looking letters
giving us the expectation
of thunder; I want an orgasm
to happen without gods. Why
define all the fun? Love me,
love me, love me, what a bore.

Now you got to buy a diamond
ring, and don't forget flowers
sheared from their roots;
smell the paper and not
the petals. See them on
the map, let us leave not
one inch to the imagination.
Let us make shapes out
of the sky to tell
the time. Let us stay
in between the lines.

Hello.

It takes
a universe to blink,
yet you do not want
to do everything
at once. You think
you do, but you don't.
You think you have
got to have
happiness and truth,
then eternity all in
an orgasm of flesh
with no friction,
no heavy breath, no
shy eyes to chase, no
fingers to trace skin
and contemplate
the beauty of it all.
Are you not asking
for much? You are
both the flame
and the rocket ship,
you are the oxygen,
the jet fuel burning
into uncertainty.

Carry on! Yes, it will
pass. Take time to say
your thank you's
and goodbyes. Then leave
to make room for the new
arrivals in the lobby.
Perhaps, if you are lucky,
they will gaze
at your monument
in the sky and admire
its size.

Hollow

I cannot hear you,
I cannot hear your art,
your philosophy,
your questions to disrupt
the illusion of my indoctrination,
my pleasures of my damnation.
I am a ghost, certainly lifeless
and breathing in a body
and little else.
Sometimes I take stints
to the Keys
to swim and drown
the loud silence of my voice
wrapped in a margarita
and a sail boat.
The Buffett music plays loud
so it is easy
to ignore the message from the Jesus
walking along the uneasy waters
with a begging cup
and tee-shirt stained
with the outlines of his ribs.
He reminds me of the next zombie flick
as my mouth waters for the irony
of its lifeless flesh. Week after week,
year after year, I forget
the language I was born with,
the language which learned,
which explored the forests,
the sand lots, the farms
with a mountain bike
mapping out the curiosity
of a twelve-year old boy.

But now as I watch the sun sinking
into the ocean,
it is nothing more than a fireworks display
to my vapid eyes, I do not see
the canvas being filled,
I do not see creation;
all I see is a stuffed world.
I can be stuffed,
and I can feign
so I can be anybody they want me to be
if it fills my stomach,
keeps me warm away from my cold,
and lets me fuck like a machine
to reproduce and spawn
with no use for love.

Machine Dreams

They are always asleep
in this poem,
not wearing any pants
dreaming of a crowd
dancing around a fire,
and in the flames
they see all
the destruction and heat
in their electric eyes
taking photographs
of:

    cities crumbling because
    of the giant lizard monsters
    shooting fire out of their nose,
    and the trading
    still takes place
    at the market,
        they still need sex
        after all;

gods now men
with strings attached
to backs, when pulled,
they say things
like
    "admire me
    and I will give
    you all your fancy clothes
    with a fancy home"
and
    "this land is free";

        wires
        closer
        to brains;

        hearts wired
        to the moving pictures
        of Hollywood, CA
        defining paradise
        with teeth
        and rainbows;

pretty girls
and boys
always winning when
they are sleeping;

        marching
        and
        whipping
        and
        marching
        and
        selling
        and
        marching
        and
        killing
        and
        marching
        and
        dancing
        and
        marching

and
fucking
and
dying;

the mobs
disconnected
 from nature,
disconnected
 from the steady beat
 inside chests,
connected
 to the invisible
 waves crashing
 into living rooms,
  they don't want to cry anymore,
  they don't want to try anymore;

magnifying glasses losing their power;

Nazis and cavemen,
Romans and priests,
the British Empire
sailing the seas
delivering the goods,
 tobacco and tea,
 rifles and slaves.

They see
it has always been
this way,
and wait for a message
from their sponsor.

 And they buy it.

life

I will start
with this: life goes on
until you are dead and still
life goes on

and everyone
is busy being practical
including
the dreamers

who dream
to speak fluent Mandarin
and have flights
that are never
cancelled

the offering

at the subway stop below Grand Central
a woman sits with a brown paper bag
full of clementines
    their sweet smell
    barely breaks through the odor
    of urine and summer
listening with wandering eyes
for the shrieks of the shuttle from Times
Square and the four through seven
    she offers one to every passerby
some look the other way and some
make small smiles and go about their afternoon

she appears to be in her mid-sixties
    she wears a heavy grey wool coat
        covering the rest of her bundled wardrobe
        over cotton stockings with soiled
        white tennis shoes
her dirty blonde hair is tied back
and she moves her jaw juttingly sometimes
    rubbing her tongue
    with her gums and the rest of her teeth

over five thousand people have passed her
by now and not one took the offer
    some threw down change
    and the occasional buck
a little boy wobbled towards her
with wide arms
    briefly outside his mother's hands
before she scooped him up and grinned
and nodded towards the old lady
with a "no thank you"
    she nodded back
    without a sound

Let Me Find Ways

Let me moan
no more words from the cyclone of images
strewn across landscapes,
in the thoughts
 between
 the beating of my heart.

Raw in breast,
struck with each gust inside me,
I search debris within.

 I wander into each storm
 with the crash of a million claps of lightening
 setting paths around me
 ablaze
 yet flames do not singe
 my bare feet.

The air,
 weighted
with ash and smoke,
covers the sky towards the fragile air:
 where the solace of titans
 embrace the heavens
 with color and mist,
 with the taste of peach and honeysuckle,
and songs of whales calling beyond the waves
 caressing and washing
 soot from toes.

I found ways
to speak tonight,
because
    I breathed with each eye
            open
    towards the creation
    past cryptic clouds
    with rays transforming
        fingers
    into scepters and swords;
    each thrust and swing, a stroke
    of paint, touch of sound
    distilling my howls into the dreams
    purging
the canvases of gods
            into human hands.

s t r e t c h

so flexible
my head can bend
around fingers
feeling the cadence
of the palette beating
from the prison
within the skin
of my breast

Every Path is the Right Path

Mission Statement

See these fingers; they will lead the march
to open the broad vista into minds of men
and women. They will not stop in the struggle
to love with words to make the doves weep
and hawks to cower into their nests. They
will fight for sands without footprints, for
the clay without form, for the empty canvas
waiting for the child within us all to turn
quiet into a sonic boom heard upon all mountains
climbed to reach the highest heaven here
on our earth. My huge strokes of courage will
aim for this, within you and within me,
they will not turn away from the face of love.

Sonnet X

My drunk eyes search not what inspires the mind,
instead they flirt upon the perfumes breathed
from loins and tongue. I hold my chest, confined

within and naked, lone with madness, sheathed
in lust with smoke of lungs without light kisses.
The sound of words are spewed to rhythmic wind

as sleep is lost where abstinence dismisses
the stars released from an ample sky skinned
into the morning alert to my quest.

And there I see the fault in numbing ways:
intoxicating love, only a guest,
a passenger, and no driver of days,

replacing blood with liquor in the heart
creating illusions to fall apart.

Sonnet XI

When eyes are closed is when finest I see;
the spinning world not in my flesh to bend
my spirit towards the masses plea
to silence my voice before I do lend
my story, my footprint left in the sand.
These words, this life I write, they are my ways
to not push but lift with my lively hand
which colors dreams, my darkness into days
and leave them in eternity. I move
until all will be black, where I will cease
to be in skin and with no more to prove;
the work complete, my heart slowed into peace
which will be carried to another mind
with more love in this spinning world to find.

Sonnet XII

Shall you not be protected by my kiss
upon the pointed hour of your desire
with hungry eyes which flutter at this,
I will renew my passion; stoke the fire
until it burns the absence of my lips.

Still danger rises to the left and right
and we feel between to hold our eclipse
obscuring history now out of sight;
surrounded in the dawns which will defend
against the bitter joys days did decline.

I dare not take you to time with no end
nor dare I question your fingers with mine,
for only fools let go of moments stronger
than an ego not at all lasting longer.

The Fountain

I am
a constant
blossoming tree
of water man made
for your amusement
and hope. You throw
your dreams in my pool,
and I know each one:
    the million dollars,
    the wants to be touched,
    the girl who smiled at you,
    and your father sleeping his shrinking
              days in a cot
              at another
              memorial.

You sit around
watching me as I
recycle your tears,
and you forget
it is of your hands
I was made to reflect
    the light of the moon,
    the stars in your eyes
    gazing from the firm benches.

You listen to the endless music
    of my pour
    comforting
    the lonesome
    as my splash
    sprays the mist
    of your wishes
    into the tangled lovers
    who once dropped their spare change
    into my well.

Light Poem

In the beginning
I asked nothing of the light,
not knowing where
it sprung from and where
it absorbed, yet
I saw and it surrounded me.

Now,
I make flames from the day,
I am an agent of the Sun.

The quantum physicists say
light is but a particle or
a wave, the eye an instrument
to turn such things into
brilliance. And philosophers
say I can only find another
through my own lit way.

From time to time, light to light
I extinguish my selfish blaze
to watch stars blanket the night.

And in this darkness you
come into my life made
of my light and shadow,
my hunger and bread, your night
found in mine. And with
each step towards
your glow, I feel your heat
and I am on fire.

The Old Folks Know

The old folks know there is no
    use in worrying;
        they know what they want,

Something warm and something sweet,
    a curious nod, a listened smile,
        the touch of skin
            upon their wrinkles.

Some have accepted old age,
    and distance to young men and women
        who stopped learning how to love.

The closest thing to an old folk
    is a child, both
        know what they want,

But old folks do not long,
    they do not cry
        for the brevity of life.

A New Home

She let
the calm wind
into her home.
She knew
it would find
its way around
the small spaces,
the breakfast nook,
the chest
containing
all the music
counting
her memories.
She knew
it would breeze
past all
the familiar
portraits
now new.

She wanted it
to hold her
and kiss
her lips,
and she found
its gust
breathing
with the water
and wine
she drank
and bathed in.

She watched
it swirl around
her back room
and cover all
her untouched
haunches
before she opened
the front door
to let it rise
back into
the air.

All the Bright Colors

See the white light,
the absence of color,
the empty brilliance
of creation waiting
for you to fill it
with all the degrees
of darkness, the shades
of your existence.

Yellow comes and it is
your friend, it warms you,
your face smiles as you
look through its translucent
cleanness. But do not be
deceived, make sure it glows
and does not give a dull stare;
otherwise its jaundiced eyes
will infect you into its hive.

Green is the color which grows,
live in it, explore it, be with
it. It can do you no harm
unless you become its enemy,
than it will whisper
to the other colors
and turn them all
against you.

Blue oversees you,
it looks down, it looks up,
it surrounds you, it reminds
you there is nothing to worry
about. It will always be there
holding you with its cool sky.
So do not try to run from its blanket
of kindness, for you will suffer
from its lonesome cold.

Brown is the color below
your feet, it supports you. Feed it
and it will feed you. Let it
be your guide, trust in its
firm trail. If you do not,
you will be lost
in its earthiness, raw,
without purpose.

Grey is the color you see
when you ignore the other
colors. Do not mind this
color and it will not mind
you.

Red is the color inside
you and it wants to get out.
It is wild, do not try
to tame it or it will tame
you and leave you with less.
Instead, hold it and love it;
it will shoot out of you,
and it will show all
of the places it lands
are inside you too.

These colors are for you,
mix them up, make new colors,
soak them up in your life,
and when it is over
they will all combine
in the incredible black
birthing a new bright white
to do it all over again.

locked to life

I can feel the sadness
in your back pocket
    folded neatly
    like a note for rum
    and sunshine

there it is
    attached to a chain
    locked to life

it falls out
    sometimes
    and hangs with your hands
    where you
    caress it,
    where you
    whisper it secrets

listen to it
    sing you to the darkness

look at it tell you

    how magnolias
    grow and fall
    from trees

    to touch the grass
    reaching for your feet

    to taste the grapes
    in your eyes

there
    silence has a melody,
    poetry has a heart,
    air dances with the children
    making shapes in the clouds

        watch their gaze,
        hold their love

and see it is all for you

Unwasted

I sing for the corpses
in the abyss, the loafers
whose smiles are never aimed
away from their own coveted eyes.
Letters enveloped never to be sent,
colors and shapes absent from
the toiled canvases; the monstrous
loves never sought.

Do they know they are alive?
Lazarus knows spears
do not point and claim dead eggs.
He is not frightened by the tongue,
the hand, the swagger of swords.
It is sin to leave the page white,
to close ourselves in our own coffin
for the living.

Shall we escape them?
Into the ark, next to the window
where we can watch the endless rains,
hear its thunder, see its rivers
swell and bursting the banks
of apathy. Do not fear the hazy
vista; the rains will pause
for the crystal sky
where we open doors
and dance to your blood and body --
and mine.

River

They swim in my movement:
they hear it rush by them
with its cool waters
to the sea, to the sky.

It wants to take them, repeat
the cycles into the rain,
into the ice-covered
peaks forming my gentle
streams, into the clouds
whispering to the soil
and the sun.

It finds ways through
landscapes, they build
their communes around me,
through me they find
their purpose, their mouth
with my mouth, their bodies
tied to my intensity.

Listen to how the wind
sings above my ripples,
and their sails cover
my perfect brokenness.

I can taste their earth,
I can feel their tiny toes
testing me before they choose
to immerse themselves into
my deep current.

I wear them as a crown
of foam as I feed their
roots, their air, their blood,
their seeds sprouting
into the love
stronger
than any river flows.

The Candle

The flicker
is in uncertain windows,
and the reverb floats
away from the middle like radio waves.

The smoke
cries into air, it rises
and stains the ceiling
in the shape of mountains.

The wax
is melted, soft, malleable,
it pushes through
the hard edge of its world.

The drips
do not find the bottom,
they harden before
they find a level spot.

Suspended in time,
they are fixed
to a temperature
that will let them fall.

Lighthouse

I knew you would come
where fog is the path
to my lantern shining
for your vessel carrying
you who lay with me
at dawn, those tangled
mornings where my heart
wants to stop time
with each beat of rising rays.

And when the day
is awake and naked, my light
no longer needed in your fire,
I will not suffer, I will be still.
Your vision guides you
through these seas now.
No longer will you look
for the gaze
of my eyes.

And still
with another broken day,
I will be here, listening
for your whistle, your cry
in your eyes staring
at the beam beneath my face
through the sneaking mist
where dusk meets a wanting body
upon restless waters.

Discovery

We cannot
wait to get
to my room
where we take
them all off:
hats, jackets,
shoes, shirts
and pants,
socks
because
we are mad
for flesh
and we are
being so discreet
about it.
Between us
the act is
anything but:
tongues in
mouths,
where they
belong;
skin moving over,
into skin,
warm skin,
skin like silk
hidden under
satin sheets.
We hide
where no one can see
our quivering,
so vulnerable
and selfless.

We look at each other
in the bedside mirror
displaying the art
of our full bodied efforts.
We are good people
doing what our parents did,
yet we believe
if we were caught by them
they would look on
with disbelief
at our naked bodies
with fright in
our delight.

Dining

I fill myself with your lips
and thirst for the hunger of
your tongue and I arrive at
your dinner again and again
as I come in overalls and then
a tuxedo in expectation and
later surprise each time I
find something new in your
slippery spout like wilderness
covered with the flavors of
berries and fog and the space
between flowers which bloom
with every glide and push
so delectable thinking I never
touched anybody else for so
long as you feel the heat from
the burner preparing the main
course waiting to be dined on
with the wide mouth of awe

a drop of water

it is rain
but it does not call itself that.
it does not call itself anything,
not water nor a drop.

it hits my face
and falls down kissing
the curve towards my neck,
and this means not one thing to it.
it does not feel as I feel it.
it could have streamed down my bedroom
window with the same feeling.

it does not even know about
heat or gravity, and how
it is in this cycle
of rising and falling,
it does not see the clouds,
the glaciers, the ocean.
its metamorphosis is unknown
to itself.

it does not know I need it,
to wet my throat,
to feed my plants.

and then time passes
and the sun
makes a rainbow.

getting up

she tires along me with dawn,
the clouds have gathered and
the rain pours and pours, we

lie close-eyed, against life,
we talk with skin, shameless,
like twin islands when moons

unite their pale sands, wave
after wave bathes our secret
bridge, retreats then pushes

until we are saturated below
the salted current broken on
each dry shore, every thrust

gets higher, dissolving into
each beach as we share grain
with grain, we open our eyes

to the day, naked, humble to
the sun, pulled towards egos
with breakfast and the daily

news, we hang a word on each
last movement until we touch
our lips and breathe the air

Can't you see me smiling?

Or do you choose to look away
where I make shadows long?
Oh, I need not tell you
of my brilliance. You have
seen it in my laughter,
in my words which breathe
and shatter mirrors
into the sand
from where
they were forged.

You knew you had
the power to ground me,
to see me weak, to hold
my aching wings
in your arms.

But now, the wind
will take me
like a condor
to weep down
feathers
upon
your
land.

Dharma in a Bag

See all the data you collected:
the apple pies, the children's
stories, Charlotte making her
web, the I love you's and cold
shoulders, the promises of
sunshine in the rain.

See how you color them all in:
the missing pieces, the variables,
the what am I supposed to be's,
the worries breaking the waves
on the shore standing on the edge
of time.

Every path is the right path. See
those clouds over your head
moving. They are all different shapes,
they all have different paths,
there are no runts, no alphas,
no omegas, no fear of failure to make
shadows on life.

swimming lessons

you're

always

f a l l i n g

into

waters

why not learn to swim?

only a glass or a pool
can be
formed

by hands
of men; but you
desire
the rivers and oceans

I tell you
stop
    holding on

let
the currents
carry you
to the
shores
of every land, of every cavern
        before unclosed eyes

be the waters,

let them unfold you,

only then
will you

move

wherever
your hands will guide you

listen
to it speak
of its dreams
and path

to you

succumb
to the language
of its cycle

like

fish to tides,
tides
to the course of moons

weave

and give to the waters

holding
you

like a net, a womb
of grain
and fruit,
lumber
    and cloth

the perpetual passage

through
the waters' power

reminds you of your own:

its murmur,
      a symphony of ripples

as you begin

to unweave

and release
      into love

Open Letter

For you,

    I write these words,
        again and again,
    this kaleidoscope
        of unspoken
            midnight talks.
This letter which seeks
    to find the world
           in your eyes.
    Because now,
        see how these words
pass you
    pulling music
    in lonesome stoplights,
        with the stereo piano
            coloring
                the sigh in your breasts
            below
            the ocean of light
            pouring
            bourbon and beer.

    You,
        who assume these certain notions
            are for your gaze alone,
            do you not see my open hand to accept
            only another of a bohemian spirit?

Better would be the doubtless laughs and walks
    towards certain dances
    having no reaction
    needed
        other than to go on to make
                      the next footprint
                          in the earth
                              bleeding
                              time.

And I will pursue
    my journey
away
    from you
    or towards you,
                           towards she who will be free
and not shut
her mouth to
            the air of my love.

                              Robert

walk to walk

you are already there
    when you walk to walk

Made in the USA
Charleston, SC
16 December 2015